Royal
Scottish
Geographical
Society

HORRIBLE GEOGRAPHY

Stunning SCOTLAND

OH DEER!

ANITA GANERI

Illustrated by MIKE PHILLIPS

SCHOLASTIC

The Royal Scottish Geographical Society is a charity registered in Scotland
No SC015599, and a company limited by guarantee No SC361477

Published in the UK by Scholastic, 2021
Euston House, 24 Eversholt Street, London, NW1 1DB
Scholastic Ireland, 89E Lagan Road, Dublin Industrial Estate, Glasnevin, Dublin, D11 HP5F

SCHOLASTIC and associated logos are trademarks and/or
registered trademarks of Scholastic Inc.

Text © Anita Ganeri, 2021
Illustrations © Mike Phillips, 2021

The right of Anita Ganeri and Mike Phillips to be identified
as the author and illustrator of this work has been asserted by them under the Copyright,
Designs and Patents Act 1988.

ISBN 978 07023 0103 2

A CIP catalogue record for this book is available from the British Library.

Printed by CPI Group (UK) Ltd, Croydon, CR0 4YY
Paper made from wood grown in sustainable forests and other controlled sources.

1 3 5 7 9 10 8 6 4 2

www.scholastic.co.uk

CONTENTS

Anita Ganeri has climbed an erupting volcano, swum through shark-infested oceans and sailed round the world solo. IN HER DREAMS! But she was born in far-away India, though she didn't realise it at the time. At school, her only interest in geography was staring out of the classroom window and working out how to escape. Since then, Horrible Geography has grown on her a bit like a mould, and she's even learned to read a map without having to turn it upside down.

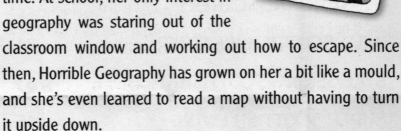

Mike Phillips was born... Yippee!! No, I mean he was born in London where he grew up and up and eventually got so big he had to leave. Which is when he discovered his love of travelling, and he set off immediately to tour the world. Nearly thirty years later he has reached North Devon where he now illustrates the entire world from a sitting position.

INTRODUCTION

Geography can be horrible. Take field trips, for starters. You've slogged for miles up a mouldy mountain. Then, you're expected to stand around IN THE FREEZING COLD, gawping at the view. Surely, it would be better to be back in your nice, warm classroom, staring out of the window*, while your geography teacher drones on and on...

*Actually, staring out the window counts as horrible geography. After all, you're watching the world go by. Bet your teacher didn't know that.

But not all geography is horribly cold and damp. It's also full of surprises. And stunning Scotland is one of them*. But forget going monster-spotting on leaky lakes. Scotland has much, much more to offer than that.

In Stunning Scotland, you can...
- visit an extinct volcano (yes, we've checked)
- go island-hopping (you'll be spoilt for choice)
- hunt down dinosaur footprints (on the Isle of Skye)
- follow in the footsteps of Scotland's greatest explorers.

*Note: if you already live in Scotland, or go there on holiday, you can skip the next bit and grab a quick nap instead. I mean, you already know Scotland's stunning. And besides, you'll need all your energy for when the exploring properly begins.

And that's not all. This book is packed with horribly interesting facts about Scotland, its stunning scenery, the people who live there, and its world-famous wildlife. This is geography like never before. And it certainly isn't boring. All you need to do is put your best walking boot forward, and set off on an awesome adventure. WAKEY, WAKEY if you've been having a kip. If you're feeling horribly lazy, don't panic. To explore stunning Scotland from the comfort of your sofa, simply keep turning the pages instead.

SENSATIONAL SCENERY

Scotland's famous for its horrible geography. I mean, it's got it all – from freaky peaks and isolated islands, to cracking coasts, leaky lochs, groovy glens and volcanoes. Yep, volcanoes. But, hang on a minute before you head off. There are a few things you need to know first.

Ask yourself:

a) where on Earth you're heading
b) what you might find when you get there
c) what you need to pack for the trip.*

RATS! FORGOT THE CANOE!

Don't worry if you don't have all the answers. This chapter's packed with Earth-shattering facts and information to keep you on the right track.

Horrible Health Warning

*This isn't fool-proof advice. Sorry. Plenty of intrepid explorers before you have got horribly lost, or left a vital bit of kit at home.

STUNNING SCOTLAND FACT FILE

Name: Scotland

AKA: Alba (in Gaelic, an ancient Scottish language. Gaelic's still spoken in some parts of Scotland, especially in the west. Scotland's main language is English.)

What is it: Scotland's a small country – it covers around 80,240 square kilometres (sq km). It's made up of a mainland and hundreds of islands.

Where is it: It's part of the island of Great Britain, in northern Europe. To the south, it's got a 154-km-long border with England. Otherwise, it's surrounded by sea water – the Atlantic Ocean, the North Sea and the Irish Sea.

SCOTLAND
IRELAND
UK

Stunning Scotland facts

- **Highest mountain:** Ben Nevis (1,345 m)
- **Longest river:** River Tay (190 km)
- **Largest loch:** Loch Lomond (70 sq km)
- **Length of coastline (including islands):** around 18,672 km
- **Biggest island:** Lewis and Harris (2,179 km)

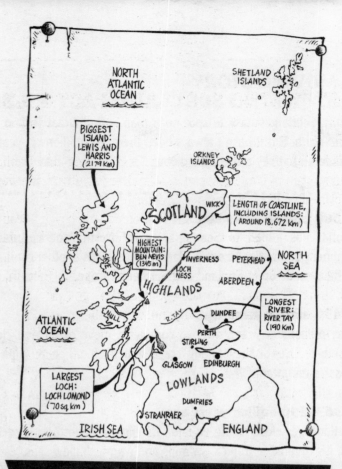

NORTH ATLANTIC OCEAN

SHETLAND ISLANDS

BIGGEST ISLAND: LEWIS AND HARRIS (2179 km)

ORKNEY ISLANDS

SCOTLAND

WICK

LENGTH OF COASTLINE, INCLUDING ISLANDS: (AROUND 18,672 km)

HIGHEST MOUNTAIN: BEN NEVIS (1345 m)

INVERNESS

PETERHEAD

NORTH SEA

LOCH NESS

ABERDEEN

HIGHLANDS

SKYE

MULL

R. TAY

DUNDEE

LONGEST RIVER: RIVER TAY (190 km)

ATLANTIC OCEAN

PERTH

STIRLING

GLASGOW

EDINBURGH

LOWLANDS

LARGEST LOCH: LOCH LOMOND (70 sq. km)

DUMFRIES

STRANRAER

IRISH SEA

ENGLAND

Earth-shattering Fact

A great gash runs right across Scotland, from the island of Arran in the west, to the town of Stonehaven in the east. It's called the Highland Boundary Fault Line, and it was created a very long time ago by movements of the Earth's cracking crust (see pages 10 to 11). It splits Scotland into two parts – the Highlands and the Lowlands. You can guess how they got their names.

A MOVING STORY

Today, Scotland's easy to spot on a map — find Great Britain and head north. But it hasn't always been there. For millions of years, it wandered happily around the globe...

c. 500 million years ago...
Scotland is joined to Scandinavia and North America, as the continent Laurentia. Across the Iapetus Ocean lies another continent, Baltica, made up of England and northern Europe.

c. 450 million years ago...
Over millions of years, the two continents move closer and closer together ... until they finally crash into each other, pushing up massive mountains.

c. 363–290 million years ago...
Scotland lies close to the equator. Its climate is hotter and wetter, and it's covered in tropical swamps and warm, shallow seas.

c. 252–201 million years ago...
Scotland's now a desperate desert, buried under giant sand dunes. Pressure forces the grains of sand together to form sandstone, a type of soft rock.

c. 66–2.6 million years ago...
Scotland's on the move again. The super-sized continent it's part of separates into Europe and North America, with the brand-new Atlantic Ocean in between.

c. 200 million years from now...

Scotland's still heading north, very slowly, and may even end up in the Arctic Ocean in 200 million years' time. It won't be part of Europe, though. It'll be part of a new continent, possibly called Amasia (America and Asia).

Earth-shattering Fact

The reason Scotland keeps drifting is 'plate tectonics'. No, not that kind of plate. These plates are gigantic pieces of the Earth's rocky crust that float on the layer of hot, bendy rock below. Heat from deep inside the Earth keeps the plates on the move.

VILE VOLCANOES

Reckon volcanoes only happen in other countries? Think again. Volcanoes can burst into life wherever there's a crack in the Earth's crust for red-hot magma to ooze through. In fact, there's evidence of volcanoes all over Scotland. But don't panic — NONE of them erupt any more.

- 6 (extinct) Volcanoes to visit.
- Arthur's Seat (Edinburgh)
- Castle Rock (Edinburgh)
- Ardnamurchan Peninsula (Lochaber)
- Ben Nevis (Lochaber)
- The Cuillins (Skye)
- Ailsa Craig (Ayrshire)

Earth-shattering Fact

Congratulations! You've reached the summit of Ben Nevis, and you've stopped for a well-earned snack. Until about 350 million years ago, though, you'd still have further to climb up. But then, this vile volcano blew its top and collapsed in on itself, knocking 600 m off its height.

ROCK 'N' ROLL

Believe it or not, every year, around twenty to thirty earthquakes shake Scotland. They happen when two plates of the Earth's crust push and shove against each other, then, suddenly, jerk apart. Luckily, you wouldn't even notice most of these tremors. Phew. But in 1880, a quake measuring 5.2 on the Richter Scale struck near Loch Awe, shaking the whole of the west coast, and neighbouring Northern Ireland.

Could you be a geologist?
There are tonnes of different kinds of rotten rock in Scotland, and horrible geographers, called geologists, spend hours studying them. But how rock-solid is your knowledge? Try this quick quiz to find out.

1. How old is Scotland's oldest rock?
a) more than 200 years
b) more than 2,000 years
c) more than 2 billion years

2. What type of rock is Torridonian sandstone?
a) metamorphic
b) sedimentary
c) igneous

3. Where did Moine schist originally come from?
a) the sea bed
b) the Moon
c) Mars

What your score means:

Award yourself ten points for each correct answer.

30 points. Top marks. You'll make a rock-solid geologist.

20 points. Not bad but you need to dig a bit deeper.

10 points and below. Oh dear. Perhaps geology's not for you. Luckily, there are plenty of experts about (see below).

FOUR GROUND-BREAKING SCOTTISH GEOLOGISTS

1. JAMES HUTTON (1726–1797)

James trained as a doctor, but became a farmer instead. He knew the land like the back of his hand, and saw that it kept changing. This gave him an idea. He reckoned natural forces deep inside the Earth were constantly at work, pushing up mountains and wearing rocks down. What's more, all of this must have happened over millions of years, which made the Earth far older than anyone realised.

14

Earth-shattering Fact

James' brainwave was extra brilliant because most people previously believed the Earth was only around 6,000 years old. This was based on Church teachings. In 1650, Archbishop James Ussher of Ireland calculated that Earth was created on 22 October 4004 BCE. Exactly.

2. HUGH MILLER (1802–1856)

Hugh came from a nautical family but his dad died in a shipwreck when Hugh was only five years old. After school, he worked as a stonemason. In his spare time, he took long walks along the coast, looking for fossils in the local sandstone rock. Among his finest finds were prehistoric fish, more than 400 million years old, with wing-like fins, and armour plating.

3. MATTHEW HEDDLE (1828–1897)

Matthew's first love was botany (the study of plants). Then disaster struck, when a (so-called) friend accidentally destroyed his precious plant collection. Instead, Matthew began collecting minerals, especially agates. Luckily, he was horribly strong and fit – handy for carrying the heavy hammers he used for bashing rocks.

4. MARIA OGILVIE GORDON (1864–1939)

Maria was born in Scotland, but moved to England at the age of eighteen. Her plan was to become a pianist, but she gave up music to study geology. In 1893, she was awarded a PhD by the University of Munich – the first a woman had ever earned. Clever Maria also spent months in the Alps on field trips, working out how mountains formed.

THREE TOP SCOTTISH PEAKS YOU WOULDN'T WANT TO MISS

Name: **Ben Nevis**
Height: **1,344 metres**

Freaky facts:
- It's the highest mountain in Scotland, and in the whole of the British Isles. In tip-top weather conditions, you can see for nearly 200 km from the summit.
- The first person (on record) to climb Ben Nevis was James Robertson in 1771. A budding botanist from Edinburgh, he was in the area collecting specimens of mountain plants.
- In 2006, during a clean-up of the mountain, parts of a piano were found near the top, buried under piles of stones.

Name: **Old Man of Storr**
Height: **49 metres**

Freaky facts:
- This small but perfectly formed peaky pinnacle sticks up from the slopes of the Storr mountain on the Isle of Skye.
- Legend says it's the stony thumb of a local giant, known as the Old Man, who once lived on the mountain somewhere.
- It's so famous it has starred in several movies, including *Snow White and the Huntsman* (2012), and *Prometheus* (2012).

Name: **Schiehallion**
Height: **1,083 metres**

Freaky facts:

• Its name means 'Fairy Hill' in Gaelic, so keep your eyes open. Apart from fairies, you might also spot red deer, brown hares, sheep, and birds like grouse and ptarmigan.

• Because of its symmetrical shape, in 1774 it was picked to be part of an experiment to work out the weight of the world.

• It's sometimes said to mark the middle of Scotland, between the country's most northerly, southerly, easterly and westerly points.

Horrible Health Warning

If someone suggests you 'bag a Munro', they're not talking about shopping. Munros are Scottish mountains over 914.4 metres tall, and there are 282 of them. They're named after Scottish mountaineer Sir Hugh Munro (1856-1919), and 'bagging' means climbing them. Sadly, Hugh didn't manage to bag them all, but he left a horribly handy list of peaks to pick.

CROOKED COASTLINE

Scotland's got A LOT of coastline, and it's a cracking place to explore. Here are some famous coastal features to spot on a stroll along the seashore.

1. OLD MAN OF HOY

You're not likely to miss this sea stack, perched off the Orkney coast. It's 137 metres tall, and made from layers of red sandstone. It was left behind when a sea arch* collapsed.

*A sea arch is made when wild waves punch a hole in the cliffs.

2. CORRYVRECKAN WHIRLPOOL

Watch out for this whopping whirlpool in the sea near Scarba. Legend says it was whipped up by a local witch. In fact, it's caused by the tides swirling around an underwater pinnacle of rock.

3. CULBIN SANDS

In 1694, a savage storm blew up here, burying homes and farms under thick piles of sand. Today, this scenic stretch of coast is covered in trees, which help fix the sand in place.

4. SMOO CAVE

Explore this limestone cave by boat or foot. You enter through its gaping mouth, into a chamber carved by the waves. Carry on into another chamber, this one worn out by rain.

5. ST NINIAN'S ISLE

St Ninian's Isle is joined to the Shetland mainland by a picturesque spit of golden sand. Horrible geographers call this a tombolo, but spit is easier to say.

Earth-shattering Fact

Another stunning Scottish seaside feature is called 'machair'. It's a mixture of grass and sand, made up of smashed seashells. It's only found in north-west Scotland (and western Ireland), and nowhere else on Earth. Try to visit in summer, when it bursts into bloom.

ISLAND-HOPPING TOUR

With around 800 islands to choose from, it could take you a while to visit them all. So, we've sent a top geographer, Sandy Beech, in your place. She's been busy posting in her travel blog:

Posted by: S. Beech

23 May at 10.03 a.m.

I'm here on the Isle of Skye, and it's a beautiful day. I'm heading for the Black Cuillin mountains - you can see their peaks for miles. If the weather holds, I'm hoping to bag a Munro or two. There are twelve to choose from along this rocky ridge.

Posted by: S. Beech

6 June at 1.25 p.m.

I caught a ferry to the Shetland Islands, in the far north of Scotland. And they're stunning. There are more than 100 islands, and I'm off to Yell (the second biggest) to do some otter-spotting. After that, it's over to Papa Stour to check out the 'Hol o' Bordie' sea cave.

Posted by: S. Beech

19 July at 6.46 p.m.

Around 200 people used to live on Hirta, the biggest island in St Kilda. Talk about hardy. They survived mostly by eating seabirds, but life was horribly tough, and in 1930, the thirty-six remaining islanders moved to the mainland. Perhaps they'd run out of recipes for gannet.

Posted by: S. Beech

30 August at 3.30 p.m.

I've hopped on this boat to Staffa, though the sea's too choppy to land. Never mind. I'm hoping to see Fingal's Cave, and the view from here's pretty good. The cave is formed from six-sided columns of volcanic rock. Or it was put there by a giant. You take your pick.

STONE THE CROWS! I NEVER KNEW THAT!

LEAKY LOCHS AND ROVING RIVERS

There are more than 30,000 lochs in Scotland, but do you know what on Earth they are? We've called on a famous lake resident to answer your questions:

ABOUT TIME, TOO!

Q: So, what is a loch exactly?
A: 'Loch' is the Scottish word for lake. A mini loch's called a 'lochan'.

Q: Are all lochs filled with fresh water?
A: No. You also get salty 'sea lochs'. They're long, jagged dents in the coastline.

Q: Which is the biggest loch?
A: It depends. Loch Lomond's the largest by area (71 sq km). But Loch Ness, where I live, holds more water than all the lakes in England and Wales PUT TOGETHER.

Q: And the largest sea loch?

A: Well, Loch Fyne's the longest. It's 64.4 kilometres from end to end. It's famous for yummy oysters, and for its basking sharks and seals.

Q: Anything else interesting to see?

A: Yes, loads. On Loch Tay, you can visit a crannog. It's a wooden house, with a pointy roof, that lake-loving people lived in around 3,000 years ago. And, in Loch Ness, there's me, of course.

Q: Okay. And if I wanted to reccy a river?

A: You can't beat the River Tay. It flows for 193 kilometres, from Ben Lui in the west, to the North Sea. It's the longest river in Scotland, and a top spot for salmon fishing, canoeing and white water rafting. So I'm told.

Earth-shattering Fact

Ever been curling? It's one of Scotland's top sports. Basically, you try to get as close as you can to a target, by sliding a heavy granite stone across the ice. And get this: it was first played on frozen lochs or rivers. Today, it's mostly played indoors.

WILD SCOTTISH WEATHER

Here's a top tip for any journey — keep an eye on the weather. Especially in Scotland. As you might know already, Scotland's weather can be, er, changeable. Not a big problem if you're popping out to the shops, but horribly risky if you're planning a long hike in the hills. Yes, it might be a nice, sunny day when you set off. But don't be fooled. The weather can quickly turn wild...

WILD SCOTTISH WEATHER FACTS

a) Sunniest place

In May 1975, the island of Tiree had 329 hours of sunshine in a month. Meanwhile, in unlucky Cape Wrath, the sun only shone for thirty-six minutes in the whole of January 1983.

b) Hottest place

Greycrook is a village in the Scottish Borders, where nothing much tends to happen. Except, that is, on 9 August 2003, when temperatures reached a record-breaking 32.9 °C.

c) Coldest place

Two places share the title for the coldest place in Scotland – Braemar and Altnaharra. On 10 January 1982 (Braemar), and 30 December 1995 (Altnaharra), temperatures dropped to -27.2 °C.

d) Wettest place

17 January 1974 was the wettest day in Scotland (so far). In just 24 hours, a soaking 238 millimetres of rain fell on Sloy Main Adit, near Loch Lomond.

e) Windiest place

The strongest gust of wind on record blasted the Cairngorms on 23 March 1986. It reached a hair-raising 278 km/h – that's as fast as a very fast car.

f) Snowiest place

The Cairngorms also hold the record for the snowiest place in Scotland. On average, it snows there on around seventy-six days a year.

COOL CLIMATE

Climate is the kind of weather a place gets over years and years. Scotland has a temperate oceanic climate. At least, that's what a horrible geographer would tell you. Roughly translated, this means Scotland has warm summers and mild winters. It's never horribly hot nor horribly cold, because it's not far from the sea. Simple, really.

CAN I TAKE MY JUMPER OFF? I'M TOO HOT IN THIS TEMPERATE OCEANIC CLIMATE!

Earth-shattering Fact

Places as far north as Scotland are usually much chillier. So, why on Earth is Scotland so toasty? It's all down to the Gulf Stream, a warm ocean current that flows from North America, across the Atlantic Ocean, and up the Scottish west coast. It keeps Scotland much warmer than it should be – warm enough for tropical plants, like plucky palm trees, to grow.

AN ICY PAST

While you're happily chilling out under a palm tree though, don't forget – stunning Scotland's climate wasn't always meek and mild...

INCREDIBLE ICE AGE FACT FILE

Name: The Ice Age

When was it: c. 2.6 million–14,500 years ago

What happened: Massive sheets of ice covered Scotland. In places, the ice was hundreds of metres thick, and only the highest peaks poked out. But it wasn't all one long, icy blast. There were cold snaps (glacials), followed by warm snaps (interglacials), followed by more cold snaps (glacials), followed by... You get the p-p-p-picture.

GROOVY GLACIERS

In the Ice Age, snow fell on the mountains and collected in hollows in the rocks. More snow fell on top, squashing the bottom layers into ice. Then, very, very slowly, the ice started to slide downhill. Time to get to grips with a glacier...

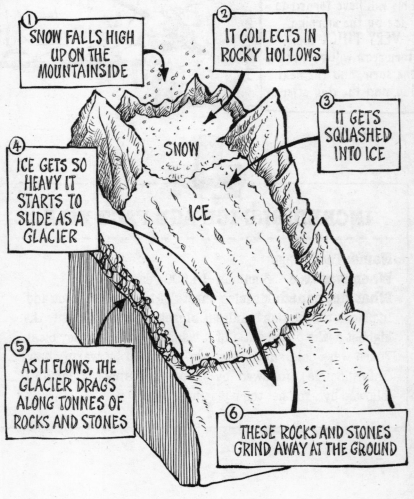

1. SNOW FALLS HIGH UP ON THE MOUNTAINSIDE

2. IT COLLECTS IN ROCKY HOLLOWS

3. IT GETS SQUASHED INTO ICE

4. ICE GETS SO HEAVY IT STARTS TO SLIDE AS A GLACIER

SNOW

ICE

5. AS IT FLOWS, THE GLACIER DRAGS ALONG TONNES OF ROCKS AND STONES

6. THESE ROCKS AND STONES GRIND AWAY AT THE GROUND

FROSTY FEATURES

All those rocky bits stuck in the ice gave glaciers a horribly cutting edge. As gritty glaciers glided along, they scraped away* at the mountainside, creating frosty features you can see all over Scotland today. Which would you be able to spot? Try this quick quiz to find out.

*Technically, this is called erosion. And it can really grind you down.

WHICH OF THESE FROSTY FEATURES WASN'T CARVED OUT BY ICE?

1. CORRIE
2. U-SHAPED VALLEY
3. DRUMLIN
4. CRAG AND TAIL
5. ARÊTE
6. RAISED BEACH

Sorry, trick question. The answer is ALL OF THEM WERE.

1. It's a hollow where a glacier starts, high up on a hillside. The ice carves it into a shape like a huge, rocky armchair, with a rocky back and arms.

- **Where to see:** the mountain Goatfell on Arran has corries – and sits above the village of Corrie!

2. It's a valley with a flat floor and steep sides. It's formed when a glacier smoothes and scrapes away at a V-shaped river valley.

- **Where to see:** Glen Coe

3. It's a small, oval-shaped hill, smoothed into shape when a glacier flows over freshly dumped rocks.

- **Where to see:** Glasgow is built on drumlins

4. They form where a glacier flows over rock that's hard, then soft. The hard rock's left as a steep 'crag', with a long 'tail' of softer rock behind it.

- **Where to see:** Castle Rock (crag) and the Royal Mile (tail), Edinburgh

5. It's French for 'ridge', and this rocky ridge is jagged like a knife. It's formed when two corries meet back to back.

- **Where to see:** the Cuillins

6. In the Ice Age, the ice was so horribly heavy, the land sank beneath its weight. When the ice melted, the land rose again, leaving some beaches perched above the sea.

- **Where to see:** west coast of Jura

Horrible Geography Hall of Fame

Name: James Croll
Born: 2 January 1821
Died: 15 December 1890

James had a rotten childhood. When he was three, his family was kicked off their croft, and his dad went to work as a stonemason. He also had to wear a hat all the time because he suffered from horrible pains in his head, which meant he was picked on at school. It didn't help that his teacher was seriously strict. Oh, and two of his brothers died young.

As soon as he could, James left school to look after his family. Then, one day, he spotted something in a shop that would change his life for ever. It was a copy of the *Penny Magazine*, published by the catchily named Society for the Diffusion of Useful Knowledge. James read it from cover to cover.

THE PENNY MAGAZINE
of the
Society for the Diffusion of Useful Knowledge.
49.] PUBLISHED EVERY SATURDAY 1835

But James also needed a job. Here are some of the things he turned his hand to:
- millwright (someone who repairs mill machinery)
- schoolboy (at the age of twenty-two, he went back to school to study algebra)
- joiner (someone who builds the wooden parts of houses, such as stairs)
- coffee shop owner • hotel manager • insurance salesman.

Unfortunately, none of these lasted for very long, but then, James had a stroke of luck. He got taken on as a janitor at a college in Glasgow. The pay was poor – a measly £1 a week – but college also threw in a house, and a supply of coal. Best of all, James got the keys to the library, and all the books he could possibly read.

James read about how top geologists thought ancient glaciers shaped the landscape. (Before this, most scientists blamed a Biblical flood.) Soon, he began writing his own books and papers. He reckoned there had been several ice ages in the past, caused by small wobbles in the Earth's orbit around the Sun. It was ground-breaking stuff for the time, and led the way for later scientists to prove the link.

Before long, James was getting letters and praise from leading scientists, even the great Charles Darwin. He was given honours and awards, including an Honorary Degree from the University of St Andrews. And, although he was forced to retire early, because of ill health, it wasn't bad for a boy who'd hated school, and cleaned classrooms for a living.

STAGGERING SCOTTISH WILDLIFE

With so much stunning scenery and great weather, it's no wonder hundreds of animals and plants call Scotland home sweet home. This makes it a wonderful place for wildlife watching, with more than 90,000 species to spot.

Horrible Health Warning

You're about to meet some awesome Scottish animals. But there's one creature you'll want to avoid. Yep, we're talking about midges, and, especially in summer, there are billions of these beastly blood-suckers about.

CHECK OUT THESE TOP TIPS FOR AVOIDING BEING EATEN ALIVE...

1. Stay indoors at dawn and dusk – that's when midges like to be out and about.

2. Plan your picnic for a windy day – midges are too lightweight to take off in a gust.

3. Wear light-coloured clothing – midges seem to prefer dark shades.

4. Cover up your arms and legs – midges love to munch on bare skin.

5. Slather on midge repellant – though midges can get used to it...

FOUR ANIMALS YOU WON'T FIND IN SCOTLAND (ANY MORE)

★ MISSING ★

HAVE YOU SEEN THESE ANIMALS?

DINOSAUR

LAST SEEN: *c* 170 MILLION YEARS AGO
NATURE NOTE: IN 2020, EXPERTS FROM THE UNIVERSITY OF EDINBURGH DISCOVERED 50 OUTSIZED FOOTPRINTS ON THE ISLE OF SKYE. THEY WERE MOST LIKELY MADE BY A LONG-DEAD TYPE OF STEGOSAURUS

WOOLLY RHINO

LAST SEEN: *c* 27,500 YEARS AGO
NATURE NOTE: WOOLLY RHINOS ROAMED SCOTLAND IN THE ICE AGE. BET THEY WERE GLAD OF THEIR THICK FUR. A TOOTH FROM A BABY RHINO, AND AN ADULT'S LEG BONE, WERE FOUND NEAR GLASGOW IN 1931

'LIZZIE'
AKA: WESTLOTHIANA LIZZIAE

LAST SEEN: *c* 345 MILLION YEARS AGO. NATURE NOTE: FOSSILS OF THIS LIZARD-LIKE CREATURE WERE FOUND IN A QUARRY IN WEST LOTHIAN IN 1988. SHE (OR HE—NO ONE KNOWS FOR SURE) IS THOUGHT TO BE THE OLDEST REPTILE EVER FOUND

POLAR BEAR

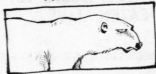

LAST SEEN: *c* 18,000 YEARS AGO
NATURE NOTE: WE'RE TALKING WILD POLAR BEARS HERE, NOT THE ONES YOU GAWP AT IN ZOOS. A PREHISTORIC POLAR BEAR SKULL WAS FOUND IN A CAVE AT INCHNADAMPH IN 1927, ALONGSIDE HIPPO AND HYENA BONES

STUNNING SCOTLAND NATURE TOUR

The best place to watch wild animals is in the wild, of course. So, you'll be pleased to know you'll be shortly setting off on your very own Stunning Scotland Nature Tour. Can't tell your red deer from your basking sharks? Don't worry — we've put together this handy nature guide. What's more, it comes with a fabulous free head net for your hat. Okay, you'll look silly, but at least you won't have midges nibbling your face*.

*For other helpful hints on what to wear, see page 33. Don't forget your camera and binoculars, whatever you do.

RED SQUIRREL
Fancy scientific name: Sciurus vulgaris

For the chance of seeing a red squirrel, head for a Scottish wood. Even if you don't spot one, you'll see signs it has been around. Red squirrels feast on nuts and pine cones, chucking their leftovers away. And, in case they fancy a snack later, they bury some grub in tree holes.

MUNCH!
MUNCH!
MUNCH!

RED DEER

Fancy scientific name: Cervus elaphus

Look out for:
• big, branching antlers (male)
• reddish-brown coat
• cream-coloured rump

Habitat: moors, mountains, woodland
Wild diet: grasses, heather, leaves, twigs
Nature note: only male deer (stags)
have antlers, which are made of
bone. They start growing in spring,
and can reach a metre across. Males
use them to fight over females (hinds),
then the antlers drop off, growing again the
following year.

When to see: year round
Where to see: Mar Lodge,
Braemar

Size (male):
• **Height:** 1.2 m at the
shoulder
• **Length:** 1.7–2.6 m
• **Weight:** 160–340 kg

BASKING SHARK

Fancy scientific name: Cetorhinus maximus

• •

Look out for:
• body longer than a bus
• massive mouth
• big, black fin on its back

Habitat: coastal waters
Wild diet: tiny sea creatures
Nature note: this whopper's the second biggest fish in the sea (after the whale shark). It swims slowly along, massive mouth wide open, taking gigantic gulps of water. It sieves out any tasty morsels of food, then squirts the water out again.

When to see: May– September
Where to see: Loch Fyne or Loch Hourn

Size:
• **Length:** up to 12 m
• **Weight:** 6 tonnes
• **Fin on back:** up to 2 m tall

ATLANTIC SALMON
Fancy scientific name: Salmo salar

· ·

Look out for:
• silvery blue with black spots (adult)
• streamlined body and pointy head
• forked tail

Habitat: rivers, sea
Wild diet: fish, squid
Nature note: this slippery fish spends most of its life at sea, but swims back to the river it was born in to lay its eggs. It doesn't let obstacles, like waterfalls, get in its way. Oh no. It simply leaps over them. Young salmon stay in rivers for a few years, then head out to sea.

When to see: year round
Where to see: rivers Tweed or Tay

Size:
• **Length:** 1.2–1.5 m
• **Weight:** the average is 4 to 6 kg. The biggest recorded to date is 40 kg

CAPERCAILLIE

Fancy scientific name: Tetrao urogallus

• •

Look out for:
• bright red ring around the eyes (male)
• bristling beard (male)
• reddish patch on breast (female)

Habitat: pinewoods
Wild diet: buds, berries, conifer needles
Nature note: male capercaillies are dreadful show-offs. To impress a female at breeding time, they fan out their tail feathers, fluff up their beards, and make a sound like a ping-pong ball. Meanwhile, females and chicks use their much duller colours to hide from predators.

When to see: year round
Where to see: Abernethy Forest or islands in Loch Lomond

Size:
• **Length:** 74–90 cm
• **Weight:** 4.3 kg (male); 2 kg (female)

OTTER

Fancy scientific name: Lutra lutra

....

Look out for:
- long, sleek body
- thick brown fur
- long, strong tail

Habitat: lochs, rivers
Wild diet: fish, crabs, water birds
Nature note: otters are brilliant swimmers. Never mind armbands, they've got webbed feet, and can shut their eyes and nose underwater. Also, their furry coats trap air to keep them warm. Otter pups (baby otters) can swim from the time they're only two months old.

When to see: year round
Where to see: Mull or centre of Perth

Size:
- **Length:** 90 cm (plus tail 45 cm)
- **Weight:** 10 kg

WILDCAT

Fancy scientific name: Felis silvestris

• •

Look out for:
- tabby-cat markings
- fluffy tail with black tip
- stocky body

Habitat: moorland, woodland
Wild diet: rabbits, birds
Nature note: congratulations if you catch a glimpse of this rare creature. Experts reckon there are only a few hundred wildcats left. They're seriously shy, and usually only come out a night. And no, your pet moggy doesn't count.

When to see: year round
Where to see: Highland Wildlife Park, Kincraig

Size:
- **Length:** 56 cm (plus tail 29 cm)
- **Weight:** 3–7 kg

STUNNING SCOTTISH BLOOMERS

Around 5,000 years ago, gorgeous green Caledonian Forest grew over Scotland. Then people began chopping down trees for firewood, wood for houses and ships, and to clear space for farmland. Soon, only a few measly fragments were left. Which was horribly bad news for animals, like bears, wolves and lynx, who lost their homes.

Over the past thirty years, people have been busy planting millions of new trees to bring the blooming forest back to life. And, if you fancy planting a Scottish forest, here are some of the best types of trees* to pick.

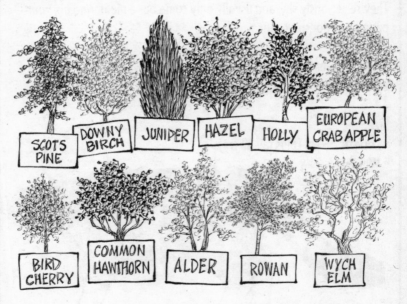

SCOTS PINE · DOWNY BIRCH · JUNIPER · HAZEL · HOLLY · EUROPEAN CRAB APPLE · BIRD CHERRY · COMMON HAWTHORN · ALDER · ROWAN · WYCH ELM

*Note: these are trees that have grown naturally in Scotland for thousands of years, so they'll fit in perfectly.

Horrible Health Warning

Trees don't just stand around in woods. They're also vital for the planet because they soak up colossal amounts of carbon dioxide. This is a ghastly gas in the atmosphere that's making the Earth worryingly warm.

SAY IT WITH... THISTLES?

A thistle has purple flowers, and long, green stems. Very pretty. But it's also COVERED IN PRICKLES*. So, why on Earth was it picked to be the national flower of Scotland? Legend says, in an ancient battle, Viking invaders wanted to creep up and surprise the Scots. They even took their shoes off so they wouldn't make too much noise. Then, one of them stepped on a thistle, and shrieked in pain. This woke up the Scots, and the plan was foiled.

*A thistle would say these are horribly useful. They protect it from being eaten.

One person who knew all about Scottish bloomers was green-fingered Patrick Geddes.

Horrible Geography Hall of Fame

Name: Patrick Geddes
Born: 2 October 1854
Died: 17 April 1932

Town planning

Patrick originally studied pestilent plants (botany) and awesome animals (zoology) but is perhaps best known as a town planner. He famously played a part in transforming the horribly dark and dismal Old Town of Edinburgh into a much nicer place to live. He even lived there himself, helping to bring people together to change the grimy old area into a vibrant community.

Patrick also had quite green fingers. He didn't think that gardening was horribly boring — he thought it was good for people's health, brought people together and helped them to learn about the natural world.

Before he died in France in 1932, Patrick took his horribly useful planning and gardening skills around the world to Jerusalem, India and Ceylon (now Sri Lanka).

"This is a green world, with animals … few and small, and all dependent upon the leaves."

SUPER SCOTTISH LIVING

Despite the soggy weather, and the risk of ending up as a midge's lunch, around 5.5 million people live in stunning Scotland. Thousands more head there on holiday, and to take in the breath-taking views.

But some parts of Scotland are easier to live in than others. I mean, how would you like to live on an isolated island, far out to sea, with no supermarkets? How on Earth would you survive, if you couldn't get a signal on your phone? In Scotland, some people are tough enough to live on islands, and they wouldn't have it any other way. But most live on the mainland, between the Highlands and the Lowlands, where there are plenty of shops to pop out to if you run out of crisps.

(EARLY) POTTED HISTORY OF THE PEOPLE OF SCOTLAND

BCE

c. 12,000

People first live in Scotland around this time. They hunt wild animals, go fishing and pick wild plants.

c. 4,000

People start growing crops, and keeping sheep and cattle. They make pottery and stone tools, as well as building huts and tombs.

c. 3,200

On Orkney, farmers build a village, called Skara Brae. Over thousands of years, it gets covered in sand. Nobody has a clue it's there until a storm in 1850 blasts some of the sand away.

c. 2,500

Bronze becomes the latest Big Thing, and people start making metal tools, weapons and jewellery. They also construct stone circles, like the one at Calanais, Lewis.

c. 700

Iron's the new heavy metal (bronze is so last year). It's harder and stronger, and weapons last for longer. People build hill forts to keep enemies (and their new improved iron weapons) away.

CE

c. 84

Julius Agricola, the Roman governor of Britain, invades Scotland or 'Caledonia' as he calls it. But he doesn't get very far, and is soon on his way back to England.

122–128

The Romans build a massive stone wall between Scotland and England, to stop the Picts (see below) heading south. It's called 'Hadrian's Wall' after the Roman emperor.

c. 400

From around 400 CE, the Picts (in the north and east), the Scots (in the west), the Britons (in the south west) and the Angles (in the south east), take control. The Picts are (probably) the most colourful because they (may have) painted or tattooed their bodies.

563

St Columba, a monk from Ireland, brings the Christian religion to Scotland. He sets up a monastery on the island of Iona.

790s

Vikings from Norway overthrow the monks on Iona. Then, instead of heading home, they settle in the northern and western isles, eventually becoming rulers of Orkney and Shetland.

WHO LIVED WHERE?

From ancient times, different settlers and the languages they spoke left their mark on Scottish words. Take place names, for starters. Can you guess who lived where? Choose from three answers:

A) PICTISH (PICTS)   B) GAELIC (SCOTS)   C) NORSE (VIKINGS)

1. INVERNESS
2. PITLOCHRY
3. LERWICK
4. KIRKWALL
5. DUNDEE
6. KINCARDINE
7. TIGHNABRUAICH
8. HELMSDALE

Answers:

1. b) 'Inver' means 'river mouth'
2. a) 'Pett' or 'Pit' means 'farm'
3. c) 'Wick' or 'Vik' means 'bay'
4. c) 'Kirk' means 'church'
5. b) 'Dun' means 'hill fort'
6. a) 'Carden' means 'thicket'
7. b) 'Tigh' means 'house'
8. c) 'Dale' or 'Dalr' means 'valley'

CITY VISITOR'S GUIDE

If an isolated island's far too far off the beaten track for you, why not live in a city instead? Pay a quick visit first, before you decide which one's for you.

EDINBURGH

Edinburgh is the capital city of Scotland, and home of the Scottish Parliament. It's a fabulous place to visit at any time, but in August, the world-famous Edinburgh Festival is well worth checking out.

Don't miss:

EDINBURGH CASTLE

• Edinburgh Castle
• The Royal Mile
• Arthur's Seat

Famous for: the scientific enlightenment and the Hogmanay celebrations

GLASGOW

Glasgow is the biggest city in Scotland, although it started off as a small village on the banks of the River Clyde. It grew into Scotland's largest seaport, and a world centre for shipbuilding, media and trade.

THE TALL SHIP

Don't miss:

• River Clyde
• The Tall Ship at Riverside
• Campsie Fells

Famous for: the friendliness of its people and a love of football

ABERDEEN

Aberdeen is on the north-east coast, and it's known as the 'Granite City' because lots of its buildings are made from local granite rock including the impressive Marischal College. It's famous today for the oodles of oil discovered in the nearby North Sea.

TH
MER
CRO

Don't miss:
- River Dee and River Don
- Aberdeen Maritime Museum
- Footdee (Fittie) fishing quarter

Famous for: its beach, the haar and its old-town university quarter

....

DUNDEE

Dundee is a must for culture-vultures. There's so much to do and see, it's tricky to know where to start. Drop in at the V&A Dundee on the waterfront, a museum designed to look like a Scottish cliff face.

DUND
LAW
MEMO

Don't miss:
- Dundee Law
- Tay Bridge
- RRS *Discovery*

Famous for: jute, jam, journalism and computer gaming

....

PERTH

Perth is known as the 'Fair City', and it has a picturesque location on the banks of the River Tay. It may be the oldest town in Scotland. One of its most famous sights is nearby Scone Palace, where the kings of Scotland used to be crowned on the 'Stone of Scone'.

FAIR MAID'S HOUSE

Don't miss:
- Scone Palace
- Fair Maid's House (HQ of the Royal Scottish Geographical Society)
- Kinnoull Hill

Famous for: renewable energy, whisky, fruit, pearls and insurance

INVERNESS

Inverness lies at the mouth of the River Ness, and is the most northerly city in Scotland. From Bronze Age graves to battlefields, its horrible history is as long as your arm.

INVERNESS CASTLE

Don't miss:
- Great Glen/Caledonian Canal
- Inverness Castle
- Nearby Loch Ness

Famous for: dolphin watching

STIRLING

Stirling is only a small city but it makes up for its size with stunning scenery. Take in the breath-taking view from the top of Stirling Castle, or the historic Wallace Monument.

Don't miss:
- Stirling Castle, tolbooth and old town jail
- Bannockburn
- Nearby Argaty red kites
- Nearby Loch Lomond & The Trossachs National Park

WALLACE MONUMENT

Famous for: over half of Scotland's population lives within an hour of the city.

FIVE SMASHING FACTS ABOUT FARMING IN SCOTLAND

1. The first farms sprang up in Scotland from around 6,000 years ago. Farmers grew grain and kept sheep and cows, but first, they had to chop down the trees to clear space for their fields.

2. By the 18th century, many farmers lived in small settlements, called 'fermtouns' ('farm towns') of up to twenty houses. They worked together in the fields around the fermtoun.

3. Today, more than three-quarters of Scotland is used for farming. But what sort of farm you have depends on whereabouts in the country you live. Rough, hilly ground is good for sheep and cattle. Lowland areas are lusher for growing crops, like barley and wheat.

4. Reckon all sheep and cattle look the same? Well, you'd be wrong. Here are a few stunning Scottish breeds, and some of their distinguishing features, to spot:

SHEEP
• Scottish Blackface: curly horns; black legs; black face
• North Ronaldsay: small size; grey, brown or red fleece; eats seaweed

CATTLE

• Highland Cattle: long, wide horns; long, red shaggy coat
• 'Belties' (Galloway Belted): mostly black with white 'belt';
no horns

5. A croft is a very small farm, and a crofter is the farmer
who works it. Each croft has its own long, narrow fields, but
it also shares grazing lands with other crofters.

Sounds idyllic. Or does it? Crofting is horribly hard work.
Could you be a highland crofter? Do you have what it takes?

HORRIBLE JOB ADVERT

TIRED OF BEING BORED TO DEATH BY TEACHERS?

FED UP WITH HAVING TO TIDY YOUR ROOM?

FANCY DOING SOMETHING COMPLETELY DIFFERENT?

WHY NOT GIVE CROFTING A GO?

YOU MUST LIKE BEING OUTDOORS IN ALL WEATHERS!

YOU MUST BE READY TO WORK VERY LONG HOURS

YOU MUSTN'T MIND LIVING IN THE MIDDLE OF NOWHERE!

HERE'S AN IDEA OF WHAT YOUR TYPICAL DAY MIGHT BE...

06.30 WAKE UP, GET DRESSED

06.45 TAKE DOGS OUT. FEED ANIMALS

09.00 EAT BREAKFAST

09.30 COLLECT FIREWOOD FROM FOREST

10.30 PICK SOME VEGETABLES

11.30 CHOP UP FIREWOOD FOR STOVE

12.30 EAT LUNCH

13.00 FIX BROKEN FENCES

14.00 SPREAD SEAWEED ON THE FIELDS

15.00 COLLECT HEAVY STONES TO BUILD A DRY STONE DYKE

16.00 FINISH WHITEWASHING THE HOUSE

18.00 CHECK ON THE ANIMALS

20.00 EAT DINNER

22.00 GO TO BED

FIVE FANCY FACTS ABOUT FISHING IN SCOTLAND

1. With all that coastline, fishing's always been part of Scottish life. Prehistoric people were particularly fond of shellfish — they left massive piles of leftover shells behind. Piles of these shells are called 'middens' and are very helpful for horrible archaeologists!

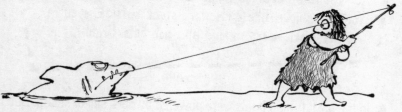

2. By the Middle Ages, people were catching so many fish, they sold any spare stocks abroad. Small fishing villages, called 'fishertouns', sprang up along the coast.

3. Diners in Europe couldn't get enough Scottish herring. By the early 1900s, thousands of fishing boats were heading out to sea, and millions of tonnes of fish were being sent abroad.

Horrible Health Warning

Herring goes off very quickly. So, as soon as a catch landed, girls called 'herring lasses' set to work gutting, salting, then packing the fish in barrels. It wasn't a job for the faint-hearted (or if you only like a fish supper for the chips). The girls were stuck outside, even in winter, ankle-deep in mud and fish guts. Urgh!

4. In the past, fishing boats were powered by oars, sail or steam. But modern boats are much more high-tech. They're kitted out with powerful engines, on-board refrigerators, and the latest electronic gadgets for navigating, and locating the biggest shoals of fish.

5. In Scotland today, many salmon are raised on farms. No, not the sort with sheep. They hatch and grow in tanks on land, then they're moved to floating cages in a (freshwater) loch. When they're around a year old, they're transferred to the sea.

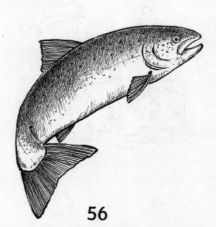

FABULOUS FORESTRY

Remember how Scotland was once one big forest? How you couldn't see the wood for the trees? How only fragments are left, and how today, people are busy planting more trees*?

Well, some of these new forests aren't just planted to look pretty (although the more natural ones are better for wildlife, of course). Their timber's horribly useful, too. Here's what happens:

1. Trees are planted by hand, close together to protect them from the wind.

*Note: these are mostly sitka spruce trees. They're fast-growing conifers with needle-like leaves and cones, and grow well in the cold.

2. When a tree reaches around forty years old, it's time for the chop. A lorry takes the timber to a sawmill.

3. As the older trees are felled, younger trees are planted to fill the gaps.

4. At the sawmill, the timber's turned into wood for building, furniture and loads more.

Earth-shattering Fact

Nothing is wasted. Any scraps of wood are mashed up and mixed with water. This is spread out in sheets, rolled and dried, and used to make paper and cardboard.

FOSSIL FUEL FACT FILES

Like lots of countries around the world, Scotland has traditionally burned tonnes of fossil fuels to generate electricity, and power factories, planes and cars. But what on Earth are fossil fuels, and where on Earth did they come from?

Name: **OIL AND NATURAL GAS**

How they are formed:

a) Millions of years ago, tiny plants and animals lived in the sea.

b) When they died, they sank to the sea bed and were buried under layers of sand and mud.

c) Slowly, the sand and mud turned into rock, and squashed their bodies into oil and gas.

d) The oil and gas are pumped out of the ground, by oil or gas rigs.

Fossil fuel fact:

• In Scotland, huge supplies of oil and gas were discovered under the North Sea in the 1960s. Since then billions of barrels of oil and gas have been pumped out.

Name: **COAL**

How it is formed:

a) Millions of years ago, swampy forests covered parts of Scotland.

b) When the plants in the swampy areas died, they were covered in mud.

c) Slowly, the mud-covered plants formed a highly carbon-rich layer (peat), which, underground and under pressure, turned into coal.

d) The coal is mined (dug out) from the ground.

Fossil fuel facts:

• For centuries, coal was Scotland's top fossil fuel for heating and cooking, and generating electricity. But the last coal-fired power station closed in 2016.

Horrible Health Warning

Unfortunately, burning fossil fuels has serious side effects:

• Belching out ghastly greenhouse gases – they're mainly to blame for global warming.

• Spewing out foul clouds of fumes – they poison and pollute the air you breathe.

• Running out of steam – fossil fuels won't last for ever and we're using them up fast.

THREE KINDS OF RENEWABLE ENERGY

With fossil fuels running out fast, people in Scotland are trying out new kinds of energy. They're called 'renewable' because you can keep making more of them.

1. WIND ENERGY

How it works: You need a wind turbine (a tall pole with blades). The wind spins the blades around. As they spin, they operate a generator which turns the wind's energy into electricity.

Where to see: Whitelee Wind Farm, East Renfrewshire

2. HYDRO POWER

How it works: You build a dam across a river to block its path, then let the water flow through the dam. The water spins the blades of a turbine wheel which works an electricity generator.

Where to see: Glendoe, near Loch Ness

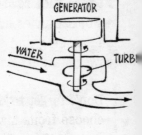

3. TIDAL POWER

How it works: You build a barrier, called a tidal barrage, in the sea which traps water at high tide. When the tide goes out, water rushes through turbines in the barrage to generate loads of lovely electricity*.

Where to see: Bluemull Sound, Yell, Shetland

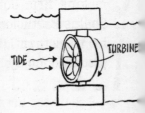

*Note: tidal energy's still in its early stages but with all that sea around Scotland, it's well worth giving it a try.

INTREPID SCOTTISH EXPLORERS

It takes guts to be an explorer, though plenty of plucky people have tried their luck. Scottish explorers have risked their lives in far-off places, determined to see the world and fill in the gaps on the maps. Some got hopelessly lost; some went mad; some dropped dead from a dreadful disease. And some even managed to get home in one piece. Fancy following in their footsteps? Well, you've come to the right place.

SURVIVAL TIP

Don't forget to take a map with you – there are loads to choose from. Many were made by famous Scottish map-making firm John Bartholomew and Son (now called Collins Bartholomew). Begun in 1826, the firm was run for more than 160 years by five generations of the same map-mad family.

RUNNING AWAY TO SEA

For years, Scottish seafarers have sailed in search of fame, fortune, adventure and... science. And what they discovered changed the course of oceanography*.

*Note: that's what suffering scientists called the study of the oceans.

Horrible Geography Hall of Fame

Name: Charles Wyville Thomson
Born: 5 March 1830
Died: 10 March 1882

A challenging voyage

In the 1870s, Charles was picked as chief scientist on the 'Challenger Expedition'. As Professor of Natural History at Edinburgh University, he was perfect for the job. A small warship, HMS *Challenger*, was fitted out as a floating science lab, and set sail on 21 December 1872. By the time it returned four years later, Charles had dredged up so many new species of deep-sea animals, it took him the next twenty-three years to write up his travel report.

Earth-shattering Fact

The Challenger Expedition was the first to make a measurement of the deepest part of the ocean. Now called The Challenger Deep in their honour, it drops almost 11 km below the ocean waves.

ADVENTURES IN AFRICA

In the 18th and 19th centuries, adventures in Africa became all the rage. It wasn't just geography that explorers had in mind, though. They were after money-making trade routes.

Horrible Geography Hall of Fame

Name: Mungo Park
Born: 11 September 1771
Died: 1806 (date unknown)

River roving

Mungo trained as a doctor. He later moved to London and joined an expedition to Africa. He set sail in May 1795, and, a year later, reached Segou (in modern-day Mali), becoming the first European to see the River Niger. Back home, he wrote a best-selling book, then, in 1805, sailed for Africa again. This time, the expedition ended tragically, when Mungo's canoe was attacked by spear-throwing locals, and Mungo himself was killed.

The grand object of my mission – the long sought-for majestic Niger, glittering in the morning sun...

Horrible Geography Hall of Fame

Name: David Livingstone
Born: 19 March 1813
Died: 1 May 1873

Quest for the Nile

David was very religious and, in 1840, he went to Africa to work as a missionary. He was soon bitten by the exploring bug. For the next thirty years, he criss-crossed Africa, despite catching deadly diseases, and being badly mauled by a lion. In 1866, he set off to search for the source of the River Nile, but fell ill. Back home, people gave him up for dead. He was finally tracked down by Welsh–American journalist Henry Morton Stanley, but refused to leave Africa.

Horrible Health Warning

David was determined to continue his quest, and in 1872 he was off again. Sadly, it was to be his last intrepid trip. Worn out by all the travelling, and seriously sick, he died on 1 May 1873. His helpers buried his heart under a tree, in African soil, according to his dying wish.

I am prepared to go anywhere, provided it be forward.

Horrible Geography Hall of Fame

Name: Joseph Thomson
Born: 14 February 1858
Died: 2 August 1895

Daring dreams

As a boy, Joseph dreamt of becoming an explorer, and often practised by sleeping outdoors. He even begged his mum to let him go and look for lost Livingstone. (He was only thirteen at the time, so she said no.) At university, Joseph studied geology. Then, one day, he saw an ad in the paper asking for people to join an expedition to Africa. Yippee! It was to be the first of many daring trips, until his death at the tragically early age of just thirty-seven years old.

> He who goes gently, goes safely;
> he who goes safely, goes far.

SURVIVAL TIP

If you find yourself in a sticky situation, try Joseph's bonkers but brilliant trick. On one of his trips to Africa, he was ambushed by unfriendly locals. But Joseph didn't fight back. Instead, he whipped out his false teeth. His attackers were so astonished, they didn't hang around.

POLAR PIONEERS

Some Scottish explorers were ready to go to the ends of the Earth... braving blinding blizzards, deep-frozen icebergs, peckish polar bears and bone-numbing cold.

Horrible Geography Hall of Fame

Name: John Rae
Born: 30 September 1813
Died: 22 July 1893

Living on ice

Born on Orkney, John signed up as a surgeon on a trading ship bound for Hudson Bay in Canada. There, he threw himself into his new life, despite the harsh conditions. He picked up vital survival tips from the local people, made his own clothes from furs and was nicknamed 'Longstride' by the Inuit for walking quickly. Later, he travelled further north to search for fellow explorer John Franklin, who had gone missing a few years before while trying to find a new sailing route.

Although my wet clothes and moccasins froze hard, I suffered no bad effect.

Earth-shattering Fact

When John died, he was buried in St Magnus Cathedral, Orkney, and honoured with a fitting stone memorial. It shows him asleep, dressed in Arctic clothes, with his trusty gun by his side.

Horrible Geography Hall of Fame

Name: William Speirs Bruce
Born: 1 August 1867
Died: 28 October 1921

Heading south

In 1892, William left university, and headed to Antarctica on a whaling ship. He later made several trips to the Arctic, before sailing south again in 1902 on the *Scotia*, as part of the Scottish National Antarctic Expedition. Over the next two years, the crew collected thousands of plant and animal specimens, and carried out important scientific experiments, despite their ship getting stuck fast in the perilous pack ice. Inspired by his adventures, once back in Edinburgh he helped establish Edinburgh Zoo and the Scottish Ski Club.

I am burning to be off again anywhere, but particularly to the far South, where I believe there is a vast sphere for research.

Horrible Health Warning

Fancy a nice plate of penguin curry? Or a steaming bowl of penguin egg soup? No, thanks? Well, you might have changed your mind if you'd been forced to camp on a windswept Antarctic island, with food rations running horribly low. Luckily, William and his crew weren't such fussy eaters, and happily tucked into their tasty treats.

Horrible Geography Hall of Fame

Name: Henry (Harry) McNish
Born: 11 September 1874
Died: 24 September 1930

Against the odds

An expert carpenter and boat-builder, Harry answered an ad for the Imperial Trans-Antarctic Expedition, led by top explorer Ernest Shackleton. He set off in 1914, on Shackleton's ship *Endurance*. Handy Harry was kept horribly busy – especially when the ship was crushed to pieces by pack ice, and finally sank. He made sure the lifeboats were seaworthy enough to survive being battered by the stormy Southern Ocean on their epic journey to get help.

> We talk of what we will eat when we get to civilisation. I myself would give a sovereign for one slice of bread and butter and two duck eggs.

Earth-shattering Fact

Harry's best friend on board was a moggy, called Mrs Chippy* (who was male). Sadly, after Endurance sank, Shackleton had Mrs Chippy shot. Harry never forgave him. But, in 2004, a life-size bronze sculpture of his precious pet was placed on his grave in New Zealand.

*Chippy is a nickname for a carpenter.

Horrible Geography Hall of Fame

Name: Isobel Wylie Hutchison
Born: 30 May 1889
Died: 20 February 1982

Journeys north

Isobel grew up in a castle. She loved going for long walks, but longed to see the world. At that time, travelling alone in a strange country wasn't considered very ladylike. But intrepid Isobel didn't care. Soon, she was off to the Arctic. First stop was Iceland, which she daringly walked across, without a map or guide. She also explored Greenland, Alaska and Canada, quietly pioneering routes across horribly inhospitable landscapes.

The things you expected to happen! Could anything be duller?

SURVIVAL TIP

On her travels, Isobel got to know the local people, and often stayed in their homes. But she didn't turn up empty-handed. For one trip to Greenland, she packed tinned haggis, tinned plum puddings and a bottle of brandy (for setting the puddings alight). Then she threw a Christmas party for the people she was lodging with.

CRAZY CLIMBERS

With all those picturesque peaks to pick from, it's no wonder Scotland has more than its fair share of mountaineers. Let's hope they've all got a horribly good head for heights.

Horrible Geography Hall of Fame

Name: William Hutchison (known as W.H.) Murray
Born: 18 March 1913
Died: 19 March 1996

Climbing high

In 1935, W.H. set off to climb his first freaky peak. He was by himself, in winter, with no maps or proper kit, and was lucky to make it safely back. But that didn't put him off. He was soon up and off again. In World War Two, he joined the army, and was taken prisoner by the Germans. After the war, he carried on climbing and writing, narrowly missing out on a place on the historic 1953 expedition that reached the summit of Mount Everest because of an injury.

From that day, I became a mountaineer.

Earth-shattering Fact

In his prisoner-of-war camp, W.H. kept himself busy writing his mountaineering memoirs — on scraps of toilet paper! Unluckily, the first copy of the book was found and destroyed by his guards, so he had to start all over again.

Horrible Geography Hall of Fame

Name: Hamish MacInnes
Born: 7 July 1930
Died: 22 November 2020

Mountain rescuer

When he was just sixteen years old, hardy Hamish climbed the Matterhorn in the Alps, which was no mean feat. He never looked back. He went on expeditions all over the world, including four to Mount Everest, despite being buried in an avalanche, and sometimes climbing in only his socks. In his spare time, he wrote books about climbing, and set up several mountain rescues. He also appeared in films as a climber, climber's double, and safety expert.

As I was going up, my feet were slipping out of the socks. It was really quite alarming.

Earth-shattering Fact

Hamish was horribly handy. In his garden shed, he invented an all-metal ice axe that wouldn't snap if a climber fell (the old kind had a wooden handle). He also designed a lightweight, folding stretcher that's now used by rescue teams around the globe.

MODERN EXPLORERS

Explorers are still setting out on hair-raising adventures to far-flung places, to find out what on Earth makes the world (and themselves) tick. Time to meet some of them.

Horrible Geography Hall of Fame

Name: Craig Mathieson
Born: 13 March 1971

South Pole success

As a young boy, Craig dreamed of skiing to the South Pole and, in 2004, he did exactly that. He covered the gruelling 1,268-km trek across the Antarctic ice in just fifty-eight days, pulling a packed sledge. On the way, temperatures plummeted to a f-f-freezing -53°C, and his friend had to pull out with frostbite. Two years later, he reached the North Pole. He was later invited to join the posh Explorers Club in New York, USA. Its other members include Ernest Shackleton, Roald Amundsen and Neil Armstrong.

> Once I knew we were going to make it, it felt absolutely brilliant and all the pain disappeared.

Earth-shattering Fact

In 2013, Craig set up the Polar Academy to help troubled teenagers by giving them a taste for exploring. But they don't just go on normal boring field trips. Oh no. They're sent off to Greenland, where they pull their own sledges, find their own way and put up their own tents on the ice.

Horrible Geography Hall of Fame

Name: Karen Darke
Born: 25 June 1971

Awesome adventures

When Karen Darke was twenty-one years old, she was left paralysed from the chest down when she fell from a sea cliff while rock-climbing. But Karen hasn't let this awful accident hold her back. In 2006, she took part in a gruelling expedition to cross Greenland. Sitting on skis, she used her arms and ski poles to pull herself 600 km over the ice. Her next awesome adventure is to sit-ski to the South Pole.

> I sometimes describe myself as an 'Explorer'... 'Explorer' is a job that never showed up in our school's career service list of suggested jobs.

Earth-shattering Fact

Karen is also a champion cyclist, riding a handbike. She won a cycling gold medal at the 2016 Paralympics. A year later, she handbiked all the way from Canada to Mexico. Awesome.

Horrible Geography Hall of Fame

Name: Polly Murray
Born: 1974

Globetrotting explorer

Polly has had horribly dangerous adventures all over the world. She's been to the Arctic and Antarctic, trekked through rainforests and was the first Scottish woman to climb to the summit of Mount Everest.

Another perilous peak Polly has conquered is Mount McKinley in Alaska, USA. When she got to the top, she skiied back down. Scary! Polly bagged the marvellous 1,083 m Munro Schiehallion when she was a measly five years old.

There were so many dangers, from polar bears to these huge ice crevasses.

Horrible Geography Hall of Fame

Name: Mollie Hughes
Born: 3 July 1990

Setting records

In 2017, Mollie broke the world record for being the youngest woman to climb Mount Everest from both the north and south sides. Three years later, she set another record for being the youngest woman to ski solo to the South Pole. She reached the Pole on 10 January 2010, after skiing 1,130 km in 650 hours, through bone-chilling cold, howling winds and a blizzard so wild and woolly, it wiped out the view for days.

I knew it would be hard but this has been an exceptionally tough experience...

SURVIVAL TIP

If you fancy following in Mollie's footsteps, make sure you pack plenty of food. To keep her energy up, Mollie had to eat around 4,500 calories every day – more than twice as much as usual. Tasty treats included choccie bars and spaghetti bolognese (freeze-dried, of course).

EPILOGUE

Congratulations! You've finished your whirlwind tour of stunning Scotland, and hopefully, you've made it back down from the Old Man of Hoy and your midgie bites are healing up nicely. But before you bore your friends silly with your holiday snaps, spare a thought for the future. Global warming's seriously turning up the heat in Scotland. It's making the weather wilder, with hotter summers and wetter winters. It's also causing the sea level to rise. The bad news is that stopping the rot isn't going to be easy. And the good news? Well, the Scottish Government, along with lots of charities and businesses, are working hard to tackle the problem before it's too late.

In 2009, after the biggest civil society campaign ever seen, the Scottish Parliament passed the strictest legislation in the world aimed at cutting fossil fuel emissions. Three years later they also launched a fund for countries affected by climate change. In 2019, having achieved the target emissions cuts early, and in part in response to the school strikes (and 15,000 school children marching on the Parliament), the targets were increased again. Scotland is proudly aiming for net zero emissions by 2045, and hoping to inspire other countries to follow suit.

The Royal Scottish Geographical Society (RSGS) has been involved throughout, and continues to try and help. It recently released an online course for students, with the University of Edinburgh, University of Stirling and the Institute of Directors to help people understand solutions to climate change.

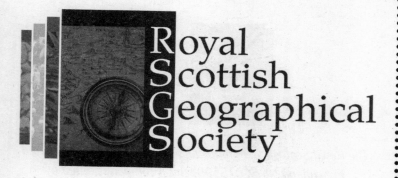

Royal
Scottish
Geographical
Society

RSGS would like to thank all those who contributed towards the costs of this publication, including:

Scottish Association of Geography Teachers
Education Scotland
The Hugh Fraser Foundation
The Gannochy Trust
New Park Educational Trust
The Russell Trust
Viewforth Trust
Descendants of John G Bartholomew
Many individual RSGS members and supporters

RSGS: a better way to see the world
– join at www.rsgs.org

The Royal Scottish Geographical Society is a charity registered in Scotland No SC015599, and a company limited by guarantee No SC361477

HORRIBLE INDEX